SHOOTING FOR GOD

USING OUTDOOR EXPERIENCES TO HONOR GOD

WRITTEN BY: AUSTIN WAGNER

ISBN: 978-1-716-26485-6

Published by Lulu Publishing.
https://www.lulu.com/

This book can be purchased on lulu.com and
many other retailers.

Cover created by Lulu Publishing

Cover photo by Karlie's Photography and Austin
Wagner
https://karlies-photography.com/

These are my memories, from my perspective,
and I have tried to represent events as faithfully
as possible. All people in this book have been
contacted and have given permission to be
represented in this book.

WRITTEN FOR ALL OF THE
CHILDREN OF GOD, TAKE
THESE STORIES AND USE
THEM IN YOUR OWN LIFE

Contents

Chapter 1

God Knows Best

Early in my life my Dad showed me what the outdoors were about— taking me hunting and fishing every chance he had. We spent hours each weekend at our 500-acre farm in Vienna, Missouri, feeding the cows and going on the occasional squirrel hunt. Dad is still an avid hunter and fisherman, spending every chance he can in the wonderful wilderness that God created thousands of years ago. He gave me passion for the outdoors through dedication and time spent outdoors together from an early age.

When I was four years old, Dad would come home from work and say, "Austin, get your hunting clothes on we have a big buck to hunt." My eyes would light up and I would run to put on my camo clothes and boots. I wanted to be just like my Dad, spending my nights watching deer and turkeys feast in our fields and hoping one would come close enough for Dad to shoot with his bow.

I remember one hunt very vividly that I will always consider the hunt that got me hooked. I was 6 or 7 years old and had been my Dad's little hunting partner for a few years already. I woke up one morning and exclaimed, "Oh my gosh! Dad! Today is the first day of archery season, can we go?"

My Dad said, "Yes, but only after you get back from school and your homework is done." I know he really wanted to say yes and take me right then.

At school, I impatiently watched the clock, for 3 o'clock all day! When the final dismissal bell rang, all I could think about was getting home and getting out in the woods. I took off like a rocket down the hallway, trying to be the first kid out the doors. I ran down the street, opened the door to our house, and yelled, "Dad I am ready to go hunting with you."

I ran into my room, changed into my camo clothing and grabbed my little five dollar bow from Walmart. The bow was a straight, white piece of plastic with a black and white paracord for the bow string. The arrows were also light-weight white plastic shafts, with plastic fletching that would slice your hand open every time you shot. I felt like a true hunter when I picked up that bow—like I could hunt anything.

Fully equipped, I flew out of my room calling, "Dad hurry up! I'm ready to go shoot a deer."

We got in the truck and Dad loaded up his bow and all his gear and head to the farm my Grandpa rented near Mt. Sterling, Missouri. We had to stop for gas and Dad sent me into the station for snacks and drinks. I got Dad his favorite soda and bag of sunflower seeds, and I got myself a fruit punch and chocolate bar. When I walked up to the counter to pay, the lady at the register said, "Oh, are you going hunting tonight young man?"

I replied, "Yes! My dad is going to take me tonight and we are going to get a big buck."

She smiled and said, "Well, good luck on your hunt."

Full of excitement, I then took the goodies back to the truck.

When we arrive at the farm, Dad tells me, "Alright son, we're going to have to be really careful sneaking into our blind so that we don't scare the deer off. Just follow right behind me and watch where you step, so you don't crunch any leaves or sticks."

I follow right behind Dad, staring at the ground, carefully planning my next step, hoping we do not run off a deer. It felt like we walked for hours, taking our time to silently get to our hunting blind. The blind sat at the edge of a large soybean field near the Gasconade River. As most hunters know, a river bottom's rich and fertile soil provides an abundance of protein and food that attract some giant whitetail deer. The bucks grow antlers larger than a 6-year-old could imagine, so as we walk, I was thinking of the huge bucks my grandpa told me live here. When we finally reached the blind, we sat down in our chairs to prepare for a long night of watching the field for deer.

I sat there with my chocolate bar looking out over that seemingly endless field for movement indicating a deer. I had my little pocket binoculars that I bought at a local garage sale around my neck. I was ready.

After waiting about 30 minutes, my dad tapped my shoulder and pointed to the tree line to our right. Out stepped the biggest doe I had ever seen, she had to weigh over 200 pounds. I started to shake, my mouth started to quiver, I turned to Dad and said, "Are you going to shoot her?"

He turned to me and said, "If she comes close enough, I will take her."

We sat there watching the doe feed her way toward our blind. 50 yards away, 40 yards away, and when she is within 30 yards, my dad said, "Don't move Austin, I'm going to shoot."

Shaking like a leaf, I pray, "Please God help my Dad make a good shot."

Dad drew back his bow and waited for the doe to turn broadside, so he can make the most ethical shot. I heard a smack as the arrow pierced through the deer's heart. She ran a few yards before crashing in the leaves.

I gave Dad a giant hug and said, "You got her Dad, you got her!" I fling open the door to the hunting blind and grabbed my plastic bow to finish the harvest. I waited outside as my Dad gathered his things to be able to clean the deer. We walked up the hill towards the bright white belly of the gorgeous whitetail doe. Dad said, "Alright get an arrow ready, I need you to help me make sure she is dead." I knocked my little plastic arrow on the string, I raised my bow, looking down the shaft of the arrow to find the right aiming point and I loosened the grip on the bow string. The arrow bounced right off her belly and into the leaves, but that moment was priceless. I could not stop smiling from the moment that arrow released from my string. Dad walked up and placed my bow on the doe and had me hold her head up for a picture. He's kept that picture as a keepsake for the rest of his life.

This story is just one of many that I have from hunting with my dad. I will share many more childhood hunting stories throughout this book. In this story, my Dad sees what is most important for me and my future. God makes sure that we are always completing the work he has planned for us before he takes us on those exciting breathtaking journeys. My Dad in this story told me I had to go to school and complete my work before I could go hunting with him. My young six-year-old brain was only focused on hunting and shooting that big buck. I had blocked out the importance of school and learning and set my sight on something not nearly as important.

I have sat through many lessons at my church, Linn Family Worship Center, that pertain to just this. One was a lesson focusing on our "spiritual blinders", meaning that we need to block out all the evil and temptations and put our focus on God.

God has a plan for us, it may not be easy, and we can find ways to honor him in each and everything that we do.

No matter how badly I wanted to skip school that day and hunt, Dad would not allow me to miss out on something that may not be important to me at the time, but he knew would be important later in life. God has everything planned out in each one of our lives all the way down to the smallest detail.

"'For I know the plans I have for you,' declares the Lord, 'plans to prosper you and not to harm you, plans to give you hope and a future'" (Jeremiah 29:11 NIV).

Chapter 2

God Never Gives Up on You

This next story takes us on an adventure that I am not so proud of. I made one of the biggest hunting mistakes of my life and I learned a valuable lesson as a result. Each one of us has made mistakes in our lives, right? But the real question should be, did we learn from them?

I just got settled into my first year of high school in the year of 2014. I was a very shy and reserved kid by this time in my life. My parents made sure that I understood the importance of school and respected the authoritative figures in my life. So, I always made it to my classes on time and rarely missed school for anything. But that was not always the case for my classmates.

By September, excitement for deer season was at its peak. Many of the Junior and

Senior boys were sharing pictures of their target buck they had on camera. And they all would discuss how to plan their hunt so that they would harvest their dream buck that year. One group would miss the first two hours of classes at least twice a week so they could hunt in the morning; putting their education behind for the thrill of the hunt.

Two long weeks after the start of archery season in Missouri, the teachers were fed up with students missing classes for hunting and not engaging in lectures. One day, my last hour teacher decided that she was going to make a point. As usual she taught for 45 minutes about class but spent the last 5 minutes lecturing on the importance of school and our futures. It seemed like time was moving in slow motion when finally, the dismissal bell rings. I stood up, along with all my classmates, and began gathering my things. I heard the teacher yell from across the room, "Hey, I am not done speaking. All of you, sit down now!"

She held us in the room seven minutes after the final dismissal bell to make her point. When she finally released us, I ran down the hall to my locker, put my belongings away, and headed for the bus.

When I arrived home, Dad was waiting for me at the door dressed in all camo ready for the woods. I grabbed my camo and my bow, and we headed for the farm. The late school dismissal made me flustered and nervous as I walked to my tree. It was in a small tree line along the edge of a soybean field. I made it to my stand finally and climbed up. I set my pack down below my feet and began ranging objects in the field around me, preparing for that big buck to show up.

After only 10 minutes, I saw a heavy ten-point buck through the glass in my binoculars. My heart began to beat faster. I began to start sweating as I saw him walking my way along the edge of the field. I had buck fever. I reached over and gripped my bow so tight my knuckles began to turn white. I looked up again and the buck is on a full sprint through the middle of the soybean field. I am shaking so much as I see that 17-inch spread running my way. This was the biggest buck I had ever seen on a solo hunt.

The buck began to get into range, but he is still running at me. I clipped my release to the bow string and got ready to draw back when I realized one brutal mistake— I had forgot to nock an arrow. I sat in my tree as I watched what could have been my biggest buck I had killed yet feed 5 yards below me. I tried to slowly grab an arrow and nock it, with the click of the nock, the buck turned and ran. I was heartbroken. I spent years waiting for a buck like that to show up in front of me and I missed my opportunity. I made a mistake.

God watches us make mistakes a lot more costly than missing an opportunity with a deer, but at the time I thought I had ruined everything and did not want to hunt the rest of the year. One mistake and I was ready to give up. What if God thought like that? What if after one mistake God gave up on us? We would not be living here today if that were the case. God is forgiving and never gives up on us, no matter the mistakes we make.

"But you, Lord, are a compassionate and gracious God, slow to anger, abounding in love and faithfulness" (Psalms 86:15 NIV).

Jesus died on the cross for our sins so our mistakes can be forgiven before God. The

Bible says that we are to ask our Father in heaven to forgive us for the sins we have committed, but we must vow to never commit them again. We must learn from our mistakes and never do them again. In this hunt I learned a valuable lesson, to always nock an arrow as soon as you get in the stand. Now, I still nock an arrow as soon as I get to the stand or blind because I never want to make that mistake again. We should follow the same principles in our walk with God. When we make a mistake or sin against God, ask for forgiveness and learn from our mistake. Our eternal spiritual life is far more important than this short life we live on Earth. We cannot allow ourselves to be stuck living in this world on Earth. But instead, we should be focused on our salvation and eternal life after our flesh decays here on this Earth.

The next time you make a mistake, take the time to ask for forgiveness and begin learning how to avoid making the mistake again. Our God is forgiving and wants to see us seated by him one day in heaven.

"The Lord our God is merciful and forgiving, even though we have rebelled against him" (Daniel 9:9 NIV).

This next story is one concerning a mistake I made while turkey hunting. Now, this is by far not the first or only mistake that I have made while turkey hunting, as my dad can attest. But this one sticks out as a crucial mistake that I learned from.

One crisp spring morning, my dad and I set out to harvest our first turkeys of the season. We both had a difficult year so far and really wanted to put a turkey on the ground so we could grill some buffalo turkey strips. Dad had a spot in mind that he thinks the turkeys will be roosted so we can get an early bird. The spot is on a ridge overlooking our big bottom field. From this spot we can hear almost everywhere on the farm for that heart-pounding gobble.

We were all set up. Dad had two decoys set up on the weed-infested road and I had my 20-gauge shotgun ready in my lap. Dad began his early morning sequence of slate calls, trying to initiate a call from one of these stubborn turkeys. We sat there for about 20 minutes when we finally heard it— our first gobble! I turned and looked at Dad and whispered, "Did you hear that one?" I pointed in the direction I heard the gobble. He simply nodded and motioned for me to get up and follow him.

We slowly made our way down the hill to the bottom field, looking ahead of us with each step. Turkeys have incredible vision and can spot the slightest movement from hundreds of yards away, so each step was strategically calculated by Dad to put me in the best position to harvest this turkey. We make it down to the fence line bordering the woods and the large open bottom field. Dad says, "Alright, I want you to sit by this tree next to the fence. Don't move once you sit down because that turkey is just across the field. I'm going to walk back here and sit down and start calling to him. When he gets in range put the bead on him and shoot." It should have been simple— do not move and shoot the turkey.

I settled in at my tree, waiting for Dad to start call when I looked across the long field and saw this tiny black spot coming down the opposite hillside through the dense green of the leaves. The gobbler was coming. Dad began a small sequence of calls. The turkey gobbled and started running toward us.

I shook with anticipation. I was going to shoot the turkey so we could have buffalo turkey strips for dinner that night. I turned to look at Dad and said, "Here he comes." Unfortunately, I just made my crucial mistake. I forgot what my Dad had said just 10 minutes earlier about not moving after I sat down. I turned and I hear the turkey putting as he turned and walked the other direction. I made a mistake that cost us that turkey.

This sounds like how we are supposed to follow God. God gave us the ten commandments to follow and we are supposed to never break those commandments to honor God. We are all sinners, but God forgives us for our sins if we ask for forgiveness. Our path as Christians may sound easy at first, but as soon as you start to change your life to follow him things may become difficult.

Such as, trying to cut out using vulgar language from your life, it may be hard and take work to change. Trying to find "clean" entertainment is becoming increasingly more difficult. Cutting out alcohol from your life can be extremely hard when all your friends say, "Oh come on, one drink will not hurt you." Well, that one drink could in fact hurt you in the flesh and spiritually. But never give up! God will take all your hurt and burdens then allow you to be reborn free from those sins. You must be willing to give him those chains.

Our walk with God is difficult and we will all make mistakes along the way. God gives us trials in our life so that we can overcome them and grow closer to him. God is testing you because he loves you. He needs to know that you are ready for when your friend comes up and says, "Hey, I am having some problems in my life right now. I want to learn more about how you overcame your struggles." God has a purpose in everything he does, so never get discouraged because God will never give up on you.

"He gives strength to the weary and increases the power of the weak. Even youths grow tired and weary, and young men stumble and fall; but those who hope in the Lord will renew their strength. They will soar on wings like eagles; they will run and not grow weary, they will walk and not be faint" (Isaiah 40:29-31 NIV).

Chapter 3

Our Spiritual Tacklebox

Idea Credited to Erik Brodin

Fishing is a sport that I absolutely love to do in my spare time. I have caught many large bass and even have three of them mounted on my wall. My friend Erik Brodin shared the concept of a spiritual tacklebox at our men's retreat this year which inspired these stories.

What do you need to go fishing? A rod and reel, some line, and your tacklebox. I usually carry a large backpack filled with five trays of lures and hooks to choose from. I want to be prepared to throw out everything at the fish hoping to get them to bite.

When I went fishing on July 13, 2017, I was prepared to throw out everything I had in the hopes of catching my personal best bass. The day started by me taking advantage of a rare day off over my summer break. I called up two of my buddies and asked if they could go fishing with me. Both Dalton and Kyle responded with an excited yes! We all met at my house around noon and headed out to my farm to try our luck at bass fishing. You should know that it is over 100 degrees outside and the worst time of the day for the fish to be biting.

Once we arrived at the farm we began unpacking and tying on our favorite lures. Then we spread out along the lake. I, of course, went to the honey hole first since I know the lake better than the other two. I started with my favorite lure, a black and blue football jig with a black and blue crawdad trailer, to see how the bass reacted. This setup was successful for me in the past, so I had confidence that it work again. I threw 30 to 40 casts into the brushy area with no luck, so I decided to change the lure.

My next choice of bait was a very slight color change but the same style. This black bladed jig should cause a little more disturbance under the water and attract a bite. I walked around the lake and casted at least 60 times and still had no bites.

Meanwhile, Kyle had already caught three fish, one of which was a 4-pound bass that broke his personal best bass. I walked over to him to take a picture of his new trophy fish and asked, "Hey, what are you using?" He lifted his pole and showed me an orange spinnerbait with no trailer.

I thanked him and ran back over to my tacklebox to find something similar to try. I found a football jig with a speckled orange and black skirt on it and quickly tied it on, then headed to a new spot. I looked around to make sure I would not cast over anyone else's line, I noticed that I did not see Dalton anywhere. He was in the car listening to the radio and trying to cool off. We decided we would just stay for another 5 minutes and then leave because the sun was starting to burn us up; just enough time for a few more casts.

I found a spot with barely enough room to cast between a couple trees on the far side of the lake. I put my finger on the spool and sent my lure soaring through the air. I threw it as far as I could and saw it splash into the middle of the lake. I figured I would try a new strategy, letting the lure sink to the bottom before I reeled it in. After 30 seconds, I realized my line was moving quickly to the left, so I slowly and carefully began reeling in my line until I felt tension. I knew I had a fish on the end of my line. I felt the weight pulling against my line, so I set the hook into what felt like a log. I pulled and instantly felt the sheer force behind this fish— a monster bass.

I yelled across the lake to Kyle, "Hey! I have a big one, get over here and help me!" I fought the fish harder than any other fish I had caught before. Just as I began to wonder what size fish I have hooked into, it ascended out of the water and attempted to throw my hook. I had never seen a bass this big in my life. The bass jumped three more times and each time I held my breath hoping that it would not spit out my hook. I took it easy for a little while hoping to tire it out so I could get it out of the water.

Finally, after 15 excruciating minutes, the fish approached the bank. I reached down through the thick brush and pulled out my new personal best bass. The sun reflected from its beautifully painted scales and water trickled down my hand. I finally have this behemoth in my hands.

I threw down my pole and rushed to meet Kyle who was still making his way around the lake towards me. When Kyle sees the bass, his eyes got super big and he said, "Oh my gosh that has to be over 10 pounds!" We both stood there and looked at this beautiful fish that God created. I opened its mouth to hold it and was amazed to see a bluegill tail hanging out of it. I had never seen a fish with a smaller fish still inside its mouth. I just could not believe how incredible this day was. We ran to the car and knocked on the window to get Dalton's attention. When he looked up, he was in shock looking at the biggest fish of his life. We all took pictures with it and marveled at its beauty. I finally got out the scale and weighed it— just over 8 pounds-the biggest bass I had ever caught. I mounted that bass and hung it in our office to preserve that memory.

This story demonstrates the spiritual tacklebox in many ways, starting with choosing the right lure. When you go fishing, be prepared to throw your best lures. You want to attract and get fish to bite what you throw. When we disciple for God, we also need to be prepared to give out our best advice and wisdom when we talk to others about the glory and honor it is to be a Christian. Our goal as Christians is to bring as many people to know Christ as we can, and we need to have the right lure or hook to get our fellow citizens to hold onto the word of God. When I talk with strangers or even my closet friends about God, I always start with building a relationship with them. I want them to trust me and to feel comfortable with me. Having a bond or relationship with someone creates a perfect environment for you to cast out your lure. For example, I use church events to invite them to come visit church. Maybe it is a meal that they come to and that step of getting them there is all it took for them to be hooked on God.

Sometimes you need a different lure. Maybe the meal at church did not work or they won't come with you. Don't give up; try something else. Like relating God to their life. Look for things that your friends are interested in and try explaining to them how God created the things they love in life. Make them feel like God cares for them and loves them as God loves each one of us. No matter our sins that we have committed against him he still loves us more than we could ever fathom.

"For God so loved the world that he gave his one and only Son, that whoever believes in him shall not perish but have eternal life" (John 3:16 NIV).

"But God demonstrates his own love for us in this: While we were still sinners, Christ died for us" (Romans 5:8 NIV).

The second lesson from this story is that we can learn from those around us. When I was stuck not getting any bites on my two best lures, I walked to Kyle for advice on what lures he was using that were catching and bringing in fish. Then, once I began using his technique, I caught the monster bass.

God too wants us to put our pride aside and ask others how they disciple for him. We need to be open to asking questions and learning from others. Next time you feel stuck as a disciple ask someone else for their advice on the situation. Go to your pastor and ask, "Hey pastor, I am trying to get this person to come to church and I feel stuck. Do you have any techniques that I can use to try getting them here?" Your pastor may give you new ideas. Sometimes asking questions and listening to others is the best way to learn. For example, at the men's retreat this year, I listened to the advice from the other men in the room and Erik's devotion and am using that experience to help you cast out your different God-given lures.

Third, we as Christians must maintain patience our entire lives. In the story, I was continually casting and trying in the same group of brush without a bite until I knew I needed to move on and try something else. On the other hand, Dalton gave up and went to sit in the car. If he had went to ask Kyle for his lure or went to the spot that I caught that fish, he may have been the one holding the fish. But instead, he decided he was ready to quit and leave. There were other times that Dalton caught many fish as soon as I packed my stuff up to leave, so we need to realize that we need patience, even when things do not seem to be going our way.

If we gave up every time a person did not come to know Jesus there would be no Christians in this world. Be patient and kind when trying to fulfill God's word and bringing others to know Christ. God is patient and kind to us even though we disobey and sin against him nearly every day. God forgives us and loves us even when we sin; we need to respect him and learn to never commit those sins again. We must always continue to try even when things get tough. Even when you are not getting bites, keep casting and trying new things until the right lure gains their attention.

Finally include people you can count on in your spiritual tacklebox. Kyle and Dalton accepted my last-minute invite to go fishing and got to experience one of the most memorable days of my life. Without having them both there, I probably would not have even tried fishing in that weather. But I knew I could count on them to come along with me and help me when we were there.

We all have people in our lives that we can count on and that we trust to always be there when we need them. I surround myself with people that I know will lead me in the right direction. My family, my friends, my church family, and my girlfriend push me farther in my faith. I know that if I need them, they will be there. If I needed help getting someone to church, they will help me. They have provided guidance and clarity in situations countless times in my life. Without a strong solid group of Christians by your side and holding you accountable in life, it is difficult to lead as an example to the Christian life. We all need someone who will share their lure with you. We all need someone who will step out of the car and congratulate you when you accomplish a task you badly wanted to complete. Surround yourself with people who will build you up, not tear you down.

Chapter 4

Take the Time to Research

Turkey hunting can be frustrating, but is also rewarding. Turkey hunting takes time and requires research on the birds in your area. You must find what calls they like to respond to. What areas they tend to roost and where they like to feed. All of this takes time and patience, you must be willing to work for the reward of bringing home a longbeard. This next story showcases that with the right research and dedication you can be successful and that it can make your hunt or walk with God easier.

My Dad loves turkey hunting more than any other type of hunting. Each spring he plans and researches for the upcoming season. The night before season opening in the spring of 2015, Dad was geared up to go roost turkeys so that he would know where to find them in the morning. I had basketball practice, so Dad went to the farm without me. It was getting dark, with the sun beginning to descend below the tree line while Dad patiently waited for the thunderous sound of turkeys flying up to the roost. Dad was standing along the fence line, glassing the field when he saw two turkeys walk out of the trees into the field and he knew they would be roosted there early the next morning.

At 4:30 a.m. the next morning, my alarm blared in my ear. I rolled over to hit snooze, but I knew I needed to get moving because it is Missouri turkey season opening day. I hopped out of bed and grabbed my camo. I groggily stumbled over to my boots and slipped them on before grabbing my shotgun. Dad told me all that he had seen the night before and his game plan for the morning as we drove out to the farm.

We parked far away from the field so we wouldn't spook the turkeys. Dad grabbed the calls and decoy, and we began the mile journey to the tree line. As we walked down the steep rocky hill to the bottom, Dad said he wanted me to take the first gobbler that came out. I was excited to know that I would be the one to take the shot if we got one to come close enough. As we made our way across the field in the faint glow of the moonlight, I can see the trees quickly approaching. The grass is white with frost and each step crunched beneath us. The morning was perfect.

Dad pointed out a set of trees set slightly in from the edge of the field and told me to sit on the left side closest to where the turkeys entered to roost. As daylight approached Dad began calling, trying to locate exactly where the turkeys were so we could position ourselves. After two calls, a roaring gobble echoed from the trees 50 yards from where we were sitting. I turned slightly toward the gobble so that my body would be facing him as he came off the tree. Dad called again, and again the turkey answered. I turned to Dad and he said, "We have him, just pay attention for where he flies off."

I stared intently at the treetops scanning for any movement of the turkey. Just then I heard a deep sound coming from the direction of the tree. I heard Dad whisper, "Can you hear him drumming?" I replied, "Yeah. What is that?" Dad said that when a turkey makes that sound, the turkey is asserting dominance and signaling that he is nearby. I turned toward the field and prepared my gun; the time was nearing when the turkey would fly off the roost. I heard the flapping of his wings as he descended from the woods across from me into the field below.

When he flew into the field and was 30 yards directly in front of us Dad whispered, "Shoot him!" I lined up my bead on the red of his head and pulled the trigger. The sudden boom of the shot made my ears ring. I saw the turkey flopping in the field. I was so excited, but Dad turned and said to stay still because I know there was another with him. A minute later, a loud crack sounded as another gobbler flew from the trees to see what happened to the other turkey. I heard a click as Dad turned the gun to fire and the second turkey fell to the ground.

We jumped up and hugged each other and celebrated the successful morning. We ran out to the turkeys we harvested. Dad had killed a young jake turkey, which isn't trophy turkey, but we met our desire to fill the freezer. My turkey however, had a huge body and a thick beard that was about 4 inches shorter in the middle than on the sides and the middle was bright white on the tip. I asked Dad why the beard was so unique, and he concluded that with the extremely low temperatures the night before, the turkey's beard had become frostbitten and partially broke off. The morning quickly became the most special and unique turkey hunt of my life.

In our walk with God, we also need to do the research and devote our time to him. If Dad had not scouted the night before we wouldn't have been so successful. We would have been clueless about where to start. We probably would have spent our entire morning trying to locate a turkey.

Without digging into our bibles and attending church regularly we would be lost and not know where to go next. Life without Christ leaves you lost and confused looking for the next place to step. Jesus provides a path for us to go through life without feeling lost and confused.

He will provide the answers and guide you if you are willing to trust him and honor his plan for you. The path may be long and have many obstacles, but it will have the greatest reward at the end when you see yourself walk through the gates of heaven. Each one of these stories I share would not be possible without the creator of it all. The one who sits on the throne of heaven watching over us and providing a life here on the world he created. God created both the heavens and the earth and all the creatures that reside within it. And we are all blessed to be able to witness and explore his beautiful creation.

"In the beginning God created the heavens and the earth" (Genesis 1:1 NIV).

"By faith we understand that the universe was formed at God's command, so that what is seen was not made out of what is visible" (Hebrews 11:3 NIV).

Chapter 5

Things Happen When You Least Expect It

Ever since I can remember my Dad would go to Colorado to go elk hunting. He would always go for a few weeks in September to hunt the first week or two of archery elk season. As a young kid sitting by Dad on the couch watching elk hunting shows, I would always think, "I can't wait to go elk hunting when I get older." When I was around 10 my Dad harvested his first and only bull elk. After years of hard work, it all finally paid off when he got to hang that bull on our wall. The bull was massive, with 7 points on each side. It was always a dream I had since I was younger to kill an elk as big as my Dad's to put on my wall.

In the summer of 2019, my Dad texted me that his friend, Wes, was going elk hunting in Colorado in the fall and wanted to know if I was interested in going. Once I realized he wasn't joking I replied, "Yes! I would love to go!" The rest of the summer we researched different public hunting spots in Colorado and shopped for all the gear we needed for a few days out in the woods.

In the fall, I started my second year of college at Missouri University of Science and Technology and didn't want to miss much school for the trip. My Dad's friend, Wes, who is coming on the trip with us decided that him and his son would wait to leave on the Thursday before elk opener for us to miss as little school as possible. Dad said that if we left that Thursday and drove all through the night, we would make it for opening day, and he would go out a week ahead of us to scout areas.

On the day we were leaving, I was the most excited I had ever been. I woke up around 8 a.m. and made sure my bow was all packed up in its case. I grabbed every article of clothing that I own trying to find the perfect outfits that would keep me warm on top of the mountains. Finally, I have all my clothes packed up and all the gear I needed to haul out a massive bull from the woods.

I sat all my stuff out in the garage and walked out to my little blue Scion and made the hour journey to school. I had classes from 10 a.m. until 3:30 p.m. before it was time to go elk hunting. I finished up my final class of the day and walked under all the beautiful trees changing colors on campus to my car, thinking about how in a day, instead of concrete I would have sticks and leaves beneath my feet. Each step I take would be strategic as I made the stalk on a giant bull elk. The drive home flew by because I was dreaming of all the beautiful country I was about to see.

I loaded all my clothes and gear into Wes's truck and we began on our nearly 800-

mile journey to meet up with Dad. Dad had already been at the spot scouting for fresh signs of elk so we could find them right away. Wes, Ethan, and I were only going to be able to hunt for the first 3 days of season, so we needed to find the elk fast. On the drive there, Dad called and check on how we were doing. He told us that there was not a lot of fresh signs in the places he had been, but he had jumped a giant bull one evening on the walking trail. That got me excited! Just hearing that there was a giant in the area we would be hunting made me get the shakes and we were still 300 miles from that area.

We pulled into camp about 12:30 the next afternoon, exhausted from the long drive. We unpacked our gear and rested for a couple hours before hiking into the woods for some last-minute scouting and to get familiar with the area. Our camp was set up about a half mile from the trail into our hunting area. The trail was an old cattle trail used by the local ranchers who let their cattle freely range in the mountains, so it was beaten down with cattle tracks making it nearly impossible to distinguish which tracks were elk and which were cattle. We walked about a mile down the trail before running into the small watering hole where Dad had jumped that big bull while scouting. We searched around the water source hoping to find fresh scat or tracks indicating the elk were using it frequently. We found little fresh sign, but decided we would hike there before first light in the morning and start our day there.

The first morning of elk season started for us around 4 in the morning. The smell of bacon filled the room as we prepared for our long day in the woods. I reached across to my duffle bag and grabbed my camo from it. I slipped on my hiking boots and headed to the truck to get my bow. We began the long journey to our hunting spot.

Each step on the dirt covered trail created a cloud of dust behind me. The morning was still and all that could be heard was the faint call of songbirds. We made it halfway to the waterhole when we heard our first elk bugle. The sound echoed for miles down the mountain as the bull began to bugle again. Dad was trying to locate the bull, but the sound is echoing from several directions. We made the decision to keep moving along the trail until we can find sign or pinpoint the bull's location. Just as we began to get into sight of the waterhole, there was a loud crash to our left just above the waterhole. We looked intently as we saw the tail of an elk running through the woods. The bull had come back to the spot, but we were a little too loud getting there and scared it off.

We knew the bull will not return that day, but this was the most activity we had seen, so we split up to hunt both sides of the mountain close to the waterhole. Dad and I went up the left side of the trail looking for fresh tracks left by the bull or any other elk in the area. We walked another mile up the mountain off the trail looking for beds. We came across a wallow that stunk of elk and Dad said they must have been there recently if it smelled that strongly. We stuck close to that area and searched for places where they could be bedding or trails indicating where they were traveling through. We found two more small wallows and some rubs left by bulls.

As the morning wrapped up, we headed down the mountain to meet up with Wes and Ethan to see if they had as much luck as we did at finding sign of elk. They had not found anything very fresh, so they were excited to hear that we found fresh sign and we began to make a game plan for our evening hunt.

After sitting down and eating lunch and resting for a couple hours, we decided to go back up the mountain and sit where Dad and I were that morning. Dad and I sat at the bigger wallow under a few cedar trees, while Wes and Ethan sat along a trail that connected the other two wallows. After sitting there for several hours, the sun started to set so we headed down the mountain to the cattle trail. The grass brushed up against my hips as I walked and I tried to sneak along the field edge hoping I would see the horns of a monster bull poking up through the grass, but my vision never came true as we stumbled upon the trail again.

Once we made it back to the trail, we stood and listened for bugles from nearby bulls. About 10 minutes before complete darkness, we heard a bull scream about a mile across the valley beneath us. We knew we did not have time to make it to him before dark, but now we knew where he was for our hunt in the morning. We packed up and headed to camp, excited for hunting that bull the next morning.

The next morning we woke up a few minutes earlier to eat breakfast before heading to the trail. All four of us were motivated and eager to hunt the bull from the night before. We made a game plan for getting into position before sunrise, and took off on the trail. The morning was a little cooler than the previous morning with a little stronger wind blowing. After hiking a mile and a half we reached the point in the trail where we thought we heard the bull the night before, so we slipped into the valley below us and called. The wind was blowing straight to the bottom of the valley from where we were on the trail, so we decided to walk another half mile up the trail so our scent would be on the opposite side of the bedding area.

We moved down the mountain keeping the tall aspen trees between us and the thick brush below. My adrenaline increased with each step as I knew we were getting closer to finding our next clue of the elk's location. At the bottom of the valley, we found dozens of fresh beds and tracks. The area smelled so strongly of elk we wanted to cover our nose. We knew that we had found where the herd had been the night before when we had heard that bull. Just as we set up behind some cover, we heard a bull bugle on the ridge above us. Although it sounded as if it could be a mile away, we decided to chase after it.

We made our way up the mountain out of the valley, keeping the wind in our faces so our scent didn't blow into the places we wanted to go. The mountain was steep and full of obstacles which made our hunt more challenging but meant the elk felt safe from predators. After an hour of slowly walking up the mountain, we finally reached a small open meadow below what appeared to be an old pond dam. Dad reached into his backpack and grabbed his call. He sounded a few short cow calls to see if we could get any response from the elk. A gut-wrenching scream of a bull elk sounded just over that dam in front of us. We all turned to each other in amazement as the elk were directly in front of us.

We got down on our hands and knees and began to crawl up the steep bank that separated us and the elk. As we neared the top, Dad told us to wait as he slowly crested the top and looked over the edge. He crawled back down and told us that he didn't see elk, but what we though was a pond was a giant meadow heading down into a large open valley. Now we knew the elk were just below the opposite side of the meadow in that next valley, so we began making our way along the meadow. We stayed on the right tree line so our scent would blow back into the trees instead of the valley.

As we made our way closer to the valley, we saw a small flat above where the elk were calling that has some trees for cover. We set up along these trees in this little flat and called to the elk. Wes, Ethan, and I each stood behind three trees in a line looking towards the valley. Dad stayed in the trees 50 yards behind us, calling and raking trees trying to get the bull to come closer. As Dad called one of the bulls bugled back just 100 yards down the hill from us. We still had not seen any of the elk, but could hear multiple elk walking in the valley along the hillside. As Dad continued to call the bull answered and began to get closer to us. Each call louder than the first. We readied our bows. We heard a second bull to my right answer back, causing the first bull to get aggravated and answered that bull back and walked towards it. More cow elk called below us as the bulls started fighting.

Many elk hunters dream of one day having an experience in the woods like this one. It was unbelievable, especially for my first hunt. The bulls began to separate and the first one began walking to us again calling and getting closer. He continued walking along the hill of the flat just below the edge. We didn't see him but knew he was only 50 yards away. He paced the hillside for nearly an hour and then went back down the hill to the rest of the elk and stopped calling. After 10 minutes with no response, we wondered what happened. Then we heard crashing and hooves stomping and watched at least twelve elk run out of the draw opposite of us headed back towards the pond dam. We don't know what caused them to run out, but after we called to them for another 30 minutes without any luck, we decided to sit down and eat a few apples and readjust our plan.

We sat there 5 minutes talking about how fun and exciting our morning was when Dad looked up and saw two bulls headed our way. We turned and crawled behind cover. I grabbed my bow and got ready for them to come to us. I turned to my left and saw Wes frozen with an apple in one hand and his rangefinder in the other. When we sat down to eat, he had left his bow behind a tree a few yards behind him so he could not get it with the bulls coming closer. I turned back and see the first bull getting in range. It was a wide 4x4 bull and behind him was an even bigger 5x5. I ranged a tree in front of me that was 20 yards, waiting for one of the bulls to walk by the tree. The first bull walked past the tree and was facing directly at me so I couldn't get a good shot. I am at full draw with my bow and I noticed Ethan is too. He was farther to my right had a perfect broadside shot on the 4x4.

I heard a load pop as the first bull stepped on a branch and froze. Then smack, as Ethan released an arrow on the bull and hit it perfectly behind the shoulder. The bull ran 10 yards and stopped in confusion trying to figure out what happened. I kept my focus on the second bull behind him. I was ready to release my arrow on the second bull when both bulls turned and ran. I lowered my bow. The 4x4 Ethan shot was running with nearly the entire arrow sticking out of him. The arrow had barely penetrated through the bull's skin and the bull acted like he was hurt, but not badly.

We gathered together to talk about what happened when we heard a cow call just below us on the hill. Dad slowly snuck behind a tree and began to call. As soon as he called the first time, here she came. I saw her head pop over the hill as she called back and began running directly to me. I drew my bow back when she stepped behind a tree at 20 yards and she kept coming. When she got into a spot where I could get a shot she was only 5 yards away and saw me. Before I could release an arrow, she jumped and ran 20 yards, but stopped for a brief second— enough time to shoot. As my arrow soared through the air, the cow ducked, and my arrow flew 3 inches over her back. She turned and ran back down the hill.

We were in complete awe of what just happened. I missed my cow but the experience of having that massive animal within 5 yards was incredible. That moment made the whole trip worthwhile. We talked about the bull that Ethan shot and were a little concerned that the arrow never broke into the chest cavity of the bull.

Which meant it was not a vital hit. We investigated the spot the bull was shot to see if we could see any blood anywhere. After looking for 30 minutes we never found a drop of blood anywhere. Ethan was disappointed that we could not find the bull, but we all told him how incredible it was that on our first hunt we got a shot and had such an amazing show of elk.

Even though we did not come back home with an elk, we had an incredible hunt. We got to see everything that makes elk hunting unique and exciting. I got to release an arrow at an elk, and I could not be happier with that because most people we talked to had not even seen an elk. I am lucky that I got the chance to experience the beauty of elk hunting.

God finds us when we are least expecting it and at our most vulnerable points in life. This entire story is full of unpredictable points. When we decided to go elk hunting, we had no idea if we would even see an elk the whole trip. We had no idea what to expect to see and experience while we were out there in Colorado. I was optimistic we would harvest an elk, but I had no idea what God had in store for me and the rest of us on this journey. Jesus is our guide and beacon for our lives, but each of us has a different future in store as Christians. Each of us is called to do something different to honor our God above. We do not know when God is going to put someone in front of us who needs our guidance and help. We never know what is around the next corner of life, but God knows exactly what our future holds.

God leaves us clues and sign to help guide us to his plan for us. God has a purpose behind everything that he does in our lives. He puts people in our life to help us in our journey and he puts people in our lives for us to guide.

We need to open our eyes and pay attention to what the Lord our God is trying to show us. Our job as Christians is to honor God in everything that we do, and God will help give us the opportunities to showcase his glory.

"Whether you turn to the right or to the left, your ears will hear a voice behind you, saying, 'This is the way; walk in it'" (Isaiah 30:21 NIV).

Those elk caught us at a time when we least expected them to show up. We thought the elk had left, so we took a break and closed our minds to the thought of more elk coming. In our walk with God, remember that even when we do not feel like God is there, he is still sitting right next to us waiting for you to give him the opportunity to show his glory. God is always there, but he is waiting for us to open our eyes and see him.

When we are not at church, we think no one is watching so we can do anything we want. We may think that we can listen to vulgar music in the car because we are the only ones that know. We may think that we can watch an inappropriate show when someone leaves the room. We forget that God is still with us in the car or in your room. God is always with us watching what we do. Cut out all the things in your life that dishonor God because he may show up when you least expect it.

"Whatever you do, work at it with all your heart, as working for the Lord, not for human masters, since you know that you will receive an inheritance from the Lord as a reward. It is the Lord Christ you are serving"
(Colossians 3:23-24 NIV).

Chapter 6

Allow God to Be Your Guide

When I was a freshman in high school, I began my addiction to the sport of fishing. I had always been a big fisherman but that mainly consisted of fishing in my grandparent's backyard pond. When I started to dedicate a lot of time into the sport, I began to form a list of target species of fish I wanted to catch. That list had anything from a smallmouth bass all the way up to a shark and I put a lot of time and studying into each of the many species on that list. One of my top targets was the Striped Bass or Hybrid Bass. I had found an obsession with this species after watching countless videos on the internet of people fighting them. They just seemed like the dream fish for me.

On June 6, 2020 I went on a fishing trip that I would remember for the rest of my life. Dad, Wes, Ethan, and I drove to the Truman Lake area for one of the most memorable fishing days I have ever experienced.

We unpacked our gear from the back of the truck and headed inside to see where we would be staying for the next few days. I grabbed our fishing poles and tackle bags and began to walk across the squeaky deck through the trailer door. I put my poles in the trailer and we all walked down to the guide's house.

Our fishing guide opened his screen door and greeted us. Sitting outside, we made up a game plan for what we would do the next morning. Our guide told us that he had been catching the hybrid bass near the lake dam and had found the most success with crappie near exposed trees along the lake's edges. With a new level of confidence, we were excited to meet up again and get out on the water the next day.

After a restful night, I woke up excited to check off a white bass and a hybrid bass from my fishing bucket list. The hybrid bass is a cross between a striped bass and white bass and can be huge. They are arguably the hardest-fighting fish that can be hooked into on Truman Lake.

We loaded our gear into the truck and headed to the boat ramp. I sat in the front seat, asking our guide the whole ride about what baits and tactics he uses to catch so many types of fish on the same body of water. He told me what to look for this time of year, how to find schools of fish, and about the different baits he uses to catch crappie and hybrid bass.

Once the boat was in the water, we began the short journey to our morning fishing spot. As we got closer to the lake dam, we saw boats lined up near our planned spot. We found a spot between a couple boats and dropped down our lines to the ridge below that was submerged under the water when the dam was built. The fish used that ridge like a highway, traveling along it looking for unsuspecting bait fish. Our goal was to drop our lines in front of the ridge and slowly bounce along the bottom mimicking a dying bait fish.

After only a few casts, our guide hooked into the first white bass of the morning, then another, and another. Our guide had found a school of small white bass. He directed Ethan and me to the front of the boat and showed us where to cast. Using a spinning rod with a weighted jig head and yellow crappie bait, I casted directly where I was told and waited to bounce it off the ridge. I felt a small little tug on my line and yanked my rod up in the air. I felt the weight of a small fish on the end of my line as it swam around in the water beneath me. I pulled the line out of the water and out came a keeper-sized white bass. The first white bass I had ever caught. I threw my fish in the live well and continued fishing.

Nearly every cast that morning resulted in a catch. I caught nearly 30 white bass in the hour we were on the water and the rest of the guys caught nearly the same. I switched my bait for a little larger one in hopes of catching a hybrid bass. I bit off the end of my line and picked up my rod from the boat deck, and looked on the fish finder to locate the underwater ridge so I could cast my bait along its edge.

After about 15 casts with the new bait, I felt a hard tug on the end of my line. I prepared for a fight and yanked my rod high in the air. This time what I felt on the end was heavy and it felt like I was reeling in a giant stump from the bottom of the lake. As I reeled, the fish dove and screamed drag out of my reel. Our guide reached over, tightened my drag a little, and said, "You have a huge hybrid on the end Austin. You will have to take it easy on him and be prepared for a long fight." People in the boats around us stared as I reeled in this hard-fighting fish. I reeled and reeled, then the fish would get a sudden burst of energy and bolt to the bottom trying to break free of my line. After nearly 20 minutes of fighting with this fish I knew that he was tiring out and was coming to the surface, so I told someone to get the net ready. Finally, I began seeing color below the boat as our guide dipped the net into the water and pulled out a giant hybrid bass.

I could not believe the fight that a fish of that size could put up. The fish weighed just over 6 and a half pounds and made me work harder than ever. I respected that fish's fight. It had no idea where it was going, but exerted all its energy to prevent me from catching it. We snapped a few pictures and showed it off to some of the interested boaters nearby before throwing him in the live well.

We continued fishing to catch our limit for the day. I had caught over 60 fish that morning but only kept a few of my biggest so that I wouldn't exceed my limit. Dad, Wes, and Ethan all caught their limits as well, but there were only two big hybrids in the catch. I had never had such an action-packed day of fishing.

We also need guides in our religious walk. We try to live our lives on our own and not use the guidance of God. Dad and I had been to Truman Lake many times over the years, but we never had much luck. Once we allowed a guide to take us to the right spots and use the right techniques, we had our most successful trip on the lake. Our lives need guidance and God is there to light up our path in the darkness.

"Your word is a lamp for my feet, a light on my path" (Psalms 119:105 NIV).

God is our guide to life. The Bible lays
out his rules and words as our guide. God guides
us each day. He presents us with opportunities,
protects us from harm, and gives us life here on
this earth.

Before I was saved and became a
Christian, I did not feel like I had a purpose in
life. I struggled with my identity and depression.
My life completely changed once I gave my life
to God. He showed me who I can truly be. He
opened my eyes and my heart to many wonderful
things that I had never seen earlier in my life. I
allowed God to be the guide of my life and I
fully trust him to put me where he knows I
belong.

I want you to give your life to God and
allow him to be the guide of your life. He gave
his only begotten son so that we could live a life
on this world and still be able to have a place in

heaven next to him. Jesus sacrificed his life for our sins and gave us a chance to know God the father. Break free from your chains and burdens and allow God to take control of your life. You will be amazed at the transformation that God will do in you.

"I will lead the blind by ways they have not known, along unfamiliar paths I will guide them; I will turn the darkness into light before them and make the rough places smooth. These are the things I will do; I will not forsake them" (Isaiah 42:16 NIV).